NBA Superstars 2006

by John Fawaz

SCHOLASTIC INC.

New York   Toronto   London   Auckland   Sydney
Mexico City   New Delhi   Hong Kong   Buenos Aires

PHOTO CREDITS

All images copyright NBAE/Getty Images

ISBN 0-439-78805-6

12 11 10 9 8 7 6 5 4 3   6 7 8 9 10/0

Printed in the U.S.A.
First printing, December 2005
Book Design: Angela Jun

Introduction

Superstars for a New Generation

Basketball is a team game. Five players try to put the ball into the basket more times than their opponents, which is another team of five players trying to do the same thing.

But basketball is also an individual game, one in which special players soar. Great players electrify fans, attract millions of viewers, make their teams better, and win championships. They include slashing guards such as Dwyane Wade and Steve Nash, spectacular shooters such as Peja Stojakovic and Paul Pierce, and do-everything players such as LeBron James and Kobe Bryant.

"The main thing about today is that you have more outstanding players," said Red Auerbach, who built and coached the Celtics' dynasty that dominated the 1950s and 1960s. "But the bottom line is still putting the ball in the hole. That never changes."

These 14 players are among the best at doing that, whether they put it there themselves or dish off to a teammate for an easy basket. These are the players electrifying the crowds. These are today's NBA superstars.

Dwyane Wade

A Star Is Born

For Dwyane Wade, the rise from unknown to superstar has been like one of his coast-to-coast breaks: fast and without interruption, ending with a slam dunk.

"It seemed like it happened overnight," says Wade.

Not quite overnight, but close.

At Marquette University, in Milwaukee, Wade twice led his team to the NCAA Tournament, including their first appearance in the NCAA Final Four since 1977. Marquette advanced to the 2003 Final Four with a victory over Kentucky in which Wade posted a triple-double (29 points, 11 rebounds, and 11 assists).

Among those in attendance that night was Pat Riley, president of the Miami Heat. Three months later, Riley selected Wade with the fifth overall pick in the NBA Draft.

Wade joined the Heat and quickly established himself, thanks to his great attitude and the most explosive first step in the game.

"D-Wade goes out there, gets 30, 10, and 8 [points, assists, and rebounds], and then talks about his teammates," said Heat guard Damon Jones. "He never, ever brags about himself. Do you know how rare that is?"

Wade averaged 16.2 points and 4.5 assists per game in 2003–04 to earn unanimous NBA All-Rookie honors. He led the Heat to their first playoff appearance in three seasons. Then came Shaquille O'Neal.

With Shaq in the middle and Wade running the floor, the Heat dominated in 2004–05, posting the best record (59–23) in the Eastern Conference. Wade led the team in scoring (24.1 points per game) and assists (6.8 per game).

In the postseason, he soared even more, averaging 27.4 points per game, as the Heat took the defending-champion Pistons to seven games in the Eastern Conference Finals before falling.

Now the rest of the NBA has discovered something the Heat already knew — Dwyane Wade is a special player *and* a special person. As Heat Coach Stan Van Gundy said, "He's somebody you want your kids to look up to."

Steve Nash

O Canada!

Today, Steve Nash is one of the game's best players, a dazzling passer and clutch shooter who won the 2004–05 NBA MVP Award. But his journey to NBA superstardom has been unique, to say the least.

Nash grew up in Victoria, British Columbia, a beautiful city located on an island off Canada's Pacific coast. Most Canadian kids play hockey and soccer, but Nash loved hoops. He averaged nearly a triple-double (21 points, 11 assists, and 9 rebounds per game) while leading his high school to the British Columbia championship. A player like that must have hundreds of scholarship offers, right?

Actually, no. Nash's coach sent video clips of Steve to dozens of universities in the United States, but only Santa Clara, a private institution near San Francisco, expressed any interest. After watching Nash dominate a game, Santa Clara coach Dick Davey offered him a scholarship immediately.

Nash went on to star at Santa Clara, leading the West Coast Conference (WCC) in scoring and assists as a junior (joining John Stockton as the only players to accomplish that feat) and winning WCC Player of the Year honors as a senior.

In the 1996 NBA Draft, Phoenix selected Nash with the 15th overall pick.

Despite limited playing time during his first two seasons with the Suns, Nash impressed the Dallas Mavericks, who acquired him in 1998. In 2000–01, he emerged as a star, directing Dallas's exciting offense while leading the Mavericks to four consecutive 50-victory seasons.

In 2004, the Suns came calling. With a new coach, Mike D'Antoni, and a new up-tempo offense, they needed someone to run the show. Who better than Nash? He rejoined Phoenix and helped engineer one of the greatest turnarounds in NBA history — from 29–53 in 2003–04 to the NBA's best record, 62–20, in 2004–05. The Suns averaged 110.4 points per game, the most by an NBA team in a decade.

At age 31, Nash had his best season. He posted double-figure averages in points (15.5) and assists (11.5), the only NBA player to do so in 2004–05, and his assist average was the highest in the NBA since 1995. At season's end, he became only the second player shorter than 6 feet 6 inches to be named league MVP since 1960.

At the MVP press conference, Nash said it best: "I don't think I ever dreamed about [winning the award], so I don't know what to say . . . other than I just kept trying."

Steve Francis

The Franchise

Having trouble keeping track of Steve Francis? You aren't the only one. Lightning quick and fearless, he will go anywhere on the court.

Centers and forwards are not going to scare Francis, who overcame so much to become an NBA star. His mother's job forced the family to move often, so he attended several high schools, playing basketball only during his sophomore year.

Then Steve's mother died of cancer while he was a senior in high school. With few prospects, he attended community college. There, he averaged 25.3 points per game in 1997–98, earning a scholarship to the University of Maryland.

He made the most of his opportunity, earning Second Team All-America honors in 1998–99. In the 1999 NBA Draft, the Grizzlies selected him, but the Rockets wanted him — a lot. In a huge deal, Houston traded four players and a draft pick to Vancouver. Francis, who had been nicknamed "Franchise" as a teen, was now the franchise for Houston.

And "Franchise" delivered. And how. He averaged 18.0 points and 6.6 assists per game in 1999–2000 to share the NBA Rookie of the Year Award. He raised his scoring average each of the next two seasons, and in 2003–04 Francis led the Rockets to their first playoff berth in five seasons.

In addition, Francis became one of only five players to average 15 points, 5 rebounds, and 5 assists per game in each of their first five seasons. He did all that while overcoming a foot injury and an ear disease that causes dizziness.

"Growing up, through it all, I always believed this [success] could happen to me," said Francis. "And I always knew in addition to the court skills, I needed to build character and find out who I really was. Even now, in the NBA, injuring the foot and playing with the disease, all those things are in the way, and you have to get around them to be a good player and a good person."

In 2004, Francis became the "Franchise" for the Magic, who acquired him in a trade with the Rockets. As in Houston, he faced great expectations.

"I think I can handle it," said Francis. "If you run from pressure, that's the sign of a coward, and I don't think I'm a coward."

Coward is not a term anyone could use to describe Francis, who dives for loose balls and takes it to the hoop against big men despite his slight build. Magic fans found out, as he averaged a team-high 21.3 points per game and a career-high 7.0 assists per game in 2004–05. Orlando expects even more from Franchise in seasons to come.

Kobe Bryant

L.A. Story

Kobe Bryant won three NBA titles, earned All-NBA First Team honors four times, became the first Lakers player in 30 years to average 30 points per game in a season, and won the MVP Award at the 2002 NBA All-Star Game — all before his 27th birthday. What will the next decade hold?

Bryant seemed destined for greatness from the moment he entered the NBA. His basketball education had begun at an early age: His father, Joe "Jelly Bean" Bryant, played in the NBA and (professionally) in Europe.

During those years, Kobe became fluent in Italian — and in hoops. He followed his father to practice every day, copied his moves, and imagined himself bringing fans to their feet with spectacular plays.

Today, the 6-foot 7-inch Bryant thrills fans nightly with his skills. He is one of the most complete players in the game, excelling at point guard, shooting guard, and small forward. He can score from inside or outside (he set an NBA record for most three-pointers in a game in 2003), on turnaround jumpers and dunks, and driving layups and fadeaway jumpers.

Bryant is almost impossible to defend one-on-one, in part because he can hang in the air for so long and even adjust his shot after going up. If the double team comes, he fires laserlike passes (he averaged a career-high 6.0 assists per game in 2004–05) that often surprise opponents and teammates.

Maybe Bryant's greatest talent is his ability to take over a game, especially at the end. He has come through in the clutch so many times that Laker fans have come to expect miracles, such as the three-pointer he hit in the final game of the 2003–04 season to give the Lakers the Pacific Division title.

Now Bryant faces his greatest challenge — winning an NBA title on his own. When the Lakers won in 2000, 2001, and 2002, it was the Shaq and Kobe show. But Los Angeles traded Shaquille O'Neal before the 2004–05 season. It's Kobe's team now.

LeBron James

Better Than Advertised

Great expectations surrounded LeBron James when he entered the league in 2003 as the first overall pick in the NBA Draft. So great that it seemed impossible for anyone to live up to such hype.

James, however, did exactly that. The 6-foot 8-inch star, who is equally adept with his left and right hand, excelled in almost every part of the game, from shooting to passing to rebounding.

Opponents could not match up against James, who was too quick for forwards and too tall for guards. Plus, he could stop and pop from three-point range, making him even more dangerous.

James averaged 20.9 points, 5.9 assists, and 5.5 rebounds per game in 2003–04, becoming only the third rookie to average 20 points, 5 assists, and 5 rebounds per game.

Not surprisingly, James won the NBA Rookie of the Year Award, the first Cavaliers player to win that honor and, at age 19, the youngest player so honored.

"I knew I could make an impact, but I didn't say I was going to average this many points," said James after the season. "Statistics don't mean anything to me."

James set more records during his second season. On January 20, 2005, he had 27 points, 11 rebounds, and 10 assists in a victory over Portland to become the youngest player ever to record a triple-double. Two months later, he scored 56 points against Toronto to become the youngest player ever to score 50 points in an NBA game.

Not surprisingly, James has made believers out of everyone, especially opposing players. "He is hard to guard one-on-one because he is so big and fast," said Milwaukee forward Desmond Mason. "But if you double team him, he is still just as dangerous with the pass."

James finished the 2004–05 season with averages of 27.2 points, 7.4 rebounds, and 7.2 assists per game. He became just the fifth player to average 25 points, 7 rebounds, and 7 assists per game in a season.

James promises to only get better.

"I never think about failure," he said. "Not ever. It's just something I don't do. If I believe something, I can do it."

Shaquille O'Neal

Superman

NBA superstars don't come any bigger than Shaquille O'Neal, a huge player (7-feet 1-inch, 350 pounds) on the court and a larger-than-life personality off it. After 13 seasons in the league, O'Neal remains as big a star as ever, with almost as many nicknames (Superman, Diesel, Shaq) as All-Star selections.

In 2004–05, he came to Miami and helped turn the Heat into one of the NBA's best teams. O'Neal averaged 22.9 points and 10.4 rebounds per game, helping the Heat go from 42–40 in 2003–04 to 59–23 in 2004–05.

Before that, he spent eight seasons in Los Angeles, leading the Lakers to three consecutive NBA titles (2000–02).

O'Neal is one of the most dominant of the NBA's superstar centers. He is amazingly agile for a man his size, capable of taking the ball coast to coast for a dunk. He is also very strong — so strong that no defender can stop him one-on-one under the basket.

His game includes power moves, spin moves, a soft hook shot, a turnaround shot, and, of course, his monster dunks. He goes all out, and if a play or call does not go his way, he seldom complains; instead, he quietly goes downcourt. All with an ever-present grin and a sense of fun that has made him a fan favorite.

"He's a kid out there having fun — but trapped inside a massive body," said Horace Grant, O'Neal's teammate in Orlando and Los Angeles.

"I'm happy that the fans like to see me play," O'Neal said. "I dunk hard. I slide on the floor. I get rebounds. I can dribble the length of the court. And, hey, people want to see that. If I was a fan, I'd want to come and see Shaq play, too."

O'Neal has raised his game to another level in the postseason, winning three NBA Finals MVP Awards. He averaged 30.7 points per game during the 2000 NBA Playoffs, capped by a 41-point performance in Game 6 of the NBA Finals, a victory that gave Los Angeles its first title in 12 seasons. He averaged 36.3 points per game while leading the Lakers to a four-game sweep of the Nets in the 2002 NBA Finals.

In other words, Shaq has done it all. But he still wants more, much to the delight of Heat fans, who hope that Superman can bring an NBA title (or two) to their city.

Paul Pierce

"The Truth"

Paul Pierce grew up in the shadow of the Forum, where the Los Angeles Lakers played their home games. He wanted to be like his hero, Lakers star Magic Johnson, but there seemed little chance of that ever happening to this chubby kid.

Pierce, though, stayed on the court. He perfected his shot, and he grew into his body, becoming a rugged 6-foot 6-inch, 230-pound athlete. Soon, he was starring at Inglewood High School and the University of Kansas. The NBA beckoned.

Imagine Pierce's surprise when the Boston Celtics selected him with the 10th pick in the 1998 NBA Draft. Could this lifelong Lakers fan play for the Lakers' bitter rival?

Yes, he could, and very well, as it turned out. With his outside shooting, his classic drives to the hoop, and his post-up ability, Pierce quickly became a star in Boston. He scored, he rebounded, he made his free throws. Fans loved him because he went all out at all times. He so impressed Shaquille O'Neal that he nicknamed Pierce "The Truth."

In 2000–01, he played all 82 games and posted the first 2,000-point season by a Celtics player since Larry Bird in 1987–88. It was the first of three consecutive 2,000-point seasons for Pierce.

"My strength comes from my mom," said Pierce. "Just seeing what she had to go through to raise us, she wouldn't make excuses, she wouldn't put her head down. So I guess I looked at adversity right in the eye and took it on."

In 2004–05, Pierce averaged 21.6 points per game, his fifth consecutive season with an average of 20 or more points per game. He played all 82 games for the third time in his career. He led the Celtics to their fourth consecutive playoff berth and their first Atlantic Division title since 1991–92.

Though the 2004–05 season ended with a disappointing playoff loss to the Pacers, the Celtics have reason for optimism.

"There were a lot of question marks going into the season," said Pierce. "There are a lot of positive things."

And that's *The Truth.*

Elton Brand

Brand Identity

Elton Brand is a great player. Off the court, he is an even better person. "You have to realize that your fans are going to emulate you," said Brand. "You are a role model."

Brand's role model growing up was his mother, a single parent who raised him in Peekskill, New York. "I always had everything a little kid could want," said Brand. "It was tough on my mom but she did a great job. . . . My mother instilled my work ethic in me."

When Brand first picked up a basketball, he could not even hit the rim. That quickly changed, as he helped his team win the 12-and-under championship, then led Peekskill High School to two state titles.

Brand not only hit the boards, he also hit the books, earning a scholarship to Duke. There he won the 1999 Wooden Award as the nation's top player. He went on to play two seasons with the Bulls after Chicago selected him with the first overall pick in the 1999 NBA Draft, sharing the 1999–2000 NBA Rookie of the Year Award.

Now, after six seasons in the NBA (two with the Bulls, the last four with the Clippers), Brand works just as hard as ever on his game. At 6 feet 8 inches and 265 pounds, he is the classic power forward, battling for rebounds and taking it strong to the hoop. He can also knock down a jumper.

Brand's consistency is amazing: He averaged 20 or more points and 10 or more rebounds per game in each of his five NBA seasons. He barely missed in 2004–05, averaging 20.0 points and 9.5 rebounds per game.

"He's got desire and a great work ethic," said Clippers Coach Mike Dunleavy. "Offensively and defensively, he puts it on the line every night."

Age 26 and at the top of his game, Brand has set his sights high. The Clippers are a team on the rise, and he plans to take them and his game to the next level. He also plans to have an impact off the court with his Elton Brand Foundation, which benefits children in Peekskill; Durham, North Carolina (where Duke is located); and in Los Angeles.

"I've seen guys like Magic Johnson and Alonzo Mourning raise millions of dollars for their communities," said Brand. "That's the type of thing I want to do."

Amaré Stoudemire

The Future Is Now

As a youngster, Amaré Stoudemire idolized Shaquille O'Neal. Now it's the other way around.

"I've seen the future of the NBA, and his name is Amaré Stoudemire," said O'Neal.

Stoudemire has come a long way in a short time. He did not take up basketball until he was 14, when he shot up to 6 feet 6 inches and found he could dunk. But he attended six different high schools and sat out his junior season, which hindered his development.

When Phoenix selected him with the ninth overall pick in the 2002 NBA Draft, experts described him as a "raw" talent who would need to learn the game. Apparently talent was enough — Stoudemire, standing 6 feet 10 inches and weighing 245 pounds, averaged 13.5 points and 8.8 rebounds per game to win the 2002–03 NBA Rookie of the Year Award.

And he has only gotten better. He averaged 20.6 points per game in 2003–04, and then scored 26 points per game in 2004–05 to rank fifth in the NBA and help the Suns post the league's best record.

"Every night he's doing a highlight film, literally," said Suns coach Mike D'Antoni. "There's two or three things that I have never seen on the basketball court done by him every night."

Stoudemire, nicknamed STAT (Standing Tall and Talented), continued to live up to his nickname in the 2005 NBA Playoffs. In the 2005 Western Conference Finals against San Antonio, he poured in 37 points per game. The Suns lost the series, but Stoudemire impressed everyone.

"I don't know what to do with him," said Spurs coach Gregg Popovich. "His shot is tremendous compared to what it was when he came into the league. He has got the whole package."

San Antonio forward Tim Duncan, who was assigned the task of guarding Stoudemire, could only shake his head.

"He was hitting the 15-, 18-footer like it was nothing," said Duncan. "And with his athleticism and his ability, just knowing that he's going to get even better, it's kind of scary."

Stoudemire confirms Duncan's fear — the best is yet to come.

"I grew a lot," Stoudemire said after the Suns lost to the Spurs. "My confidence level went up and my IQ as a basketball player has gotten better. There's a lot of things I can improve on. . . . My offensive game is obviously pretty good right now, but I need to work on my defense first and foremost, and that will increase my offensive game."

A scary thought indeed, at least for the Suns' opponents.

Rashard Lewis

The Quiet All-Star

As the 1998 NBA Draft began, Rashard Lewis sat nervously in the crowd. Many predicted he would be a high pick, even a lottery pick.

But that did not happen. Indeed, he did not hear his name in the first round. Lewis slipped to the second round, going to the Sonics with the 32nd overall pick.

"Probably one of the worst days of my entire life," said Lewis in 2005. "It felt like my dream was being shattered right before my eyes."

Lewis, though, refused to give up.

"The very next day when I got home, it was time to get back into the gym and go to work," he said. "I knew I had to improve."

Improve he has. He raised his scoring average in each of his first five seasons in the NBA while expanding his shooting range. He rebounded and became a better defender.

Now he is a 6-foot 10-inch forward who excels at both ends of the court. He can light up a scoreboard, as he did against the Clippers when he scored 50 points early in the 2003–04 season, but usually Lewis quietly goes about his business.

"I feel I am a good player but not one that they are always talking about [in the media]," said Lewis.

In 2004–05, however, that changed. He ranked second on the team in scoring (a career-high 20.5 points per game), third in rebounding (5.5 per game), and second in three-pointers (173). And Lewis earned his first invitation to the NBA All-Star Game.

He also emerged as a team leader for the Sonics. Quiet by nature, he found that he needed to speak up, especially during games.

"I talked to a lot of different . . . leaders of their teams," said Lewis. "Everybody I talked to, they said your team only goes as far as your leader, and I felt this year I had to be more vocal for this team to be successful."

Behind Lewis, the Sonics went 52–30 in 2004–05 and won their first division title since 1996–97. For Lewis, it is all part of his education, which is ongoing.

"I learn something new every year," he said.

Chauncey Billups

"Mr. Big Shot"

After playing for five different teams in his first five seasons in the league, Chauncey Billups wanted to settle down. Sixteen teams called when he became a free agent in the summer of 2002. He called back only one — the Detroit Pistons.

Why Detroit? Because of Joe Dumars, the Pistons' president and Hall of Fame guard and Billups's idol. In addition, the Pistons were a team on the rise, having just won their division.

It turned out to be a perfect fit. With Billups running the offense and providing physical defense, Detroit continued its ascent. He scored a career-high 16.2 points per game while helping Detroit go 50–32 and win the division title in 2002–03.

In 2003–04, Larry Brown took over as the Pistons coach, instituting a new system that changed Billups's role. Some players might have resisted; not Billups, who embraced the change and went on to post another personal best in scoring (16.9 points per game) while dishing out a career-high 5.2 assists per game.

Better yet, Detroit won its third consecutive division title and advanced to the NBA Finals, where the Pistons shocked the Lakers, four games to one. Billups averaged 21.0 points and 5.2 assists per game during the 2004 NBA Finals to win MVP honors for the series.

"There is nobody out there I like in the clutch more than Chauncey, whether it's on the free-throw line or having to make a play or make a shot," said Dumars. "Put the ball in his hands and let him make plays. He's going to make shots, find people, and make his free throws."

Billups has made so many clutch baskets in Detroit that he has earned the nickname "Mr. Big Shot." That goes along with his other nickname: "Smooth."

"'Smooth' is my nickname from the neighborhood and the one I take the most pride in," Billups said. "I love it. I think it's the confidence that I have, not being scared."

Billups's confidence spills over to his teammates and throughout the Pistons organization.

"I don't know if there has been a more clutch guy in Detroit Pistons history," said Dumars. "[He] has done it down the stretch time and time again more than anybody I've seen."

Peja Stojakovic

Pure Shooter

In 1998, when Peja Stojakovic came to the United States from Europe to play in the NBA, he did not expect to be a star.

"I was just hoping I was going to make it and have a solid career," said Stojakovic.

Fast-forward to today, and Stojakovic is unquestionably one of the top shooters in the NBA.

Growing up in Serbia, though, Stojakovic played basketball over the objections of his father, who wanted him to play soccer. The younger Stojakovic stuck with hoops, and earned a chance to play in Greece.

There he caught the eye of NBA teams, who could not resist a 6-foot 9-inch forward with the shooting touch of a guard. The Kings selected Stojakovic with the 14th overall pick in the 1996 NBA Draft, and two years later he was headed for Sacramento. He has been tormenting defenders ever since.

"If he has an open look, you're shocked that he misses," said Kings coach Rick Adelman. "He's just such a great shooter and a great scorer."

Stojakovic came off the Kings bench his first two seasons, then became a starter in 2000–01 and averaged 20.4 points and 5.8 rebounds per game. He earned All-Star selections each of the next two seasons, and in 2003–04 Stojakovic posted career highs in scoring (24.2 points per game, second best in the NBA) and rebounding (6.3 per game) to receive Second Team All-NBA honors. In 2004–05, he again topped the Kings in scoring (20.1 points per game) while leading Sacramento to its fifth consecutive season with 50 or more victories.

Not surprisingly, opponents find it difficult to match up against Stojakovic. They need guards to chase him around the perimeter, but then they are too small to defend him inside. On defense, he can play in the backcourt or down low, presenting opponents with another set of problems.

But shooting is his strength, and Stojakovic makes it look easy.

"As the years go by, you're working harder, and [you] see that you can do better if you add some things to your game," said Stojakovic. "That's what I'm trying to do — trying to reach my best."

Stojakovic has become a big star, both in the U.S. and in Europe, especially in his home country. No doubt more youngsters in Serbia will be choosing basketball over soccer — like Peja did.

Manu Ginobili

"Flat-Out Amazing"

San Antonio coach Gregg Popovich jokingly says that his hair did not turn white until Manu Ginobili joined the Spurs.

"He's just like an untamed mustang," said Popovich.

Player and coach have had to adapt since Ginobili's arrival in San Antonio in 2002. Ginobili could sink the outside jumper, but what he liked to do most was drive the lane, draw the defense, and then shoot or dish, often attempting difficult shots or reckless behind-the-back passes. On defense he liked to freelance. His game was acrobatic, athletic, and sometimes out of control.

That put him in conflict with Popovich, who stressed a team concept involving ball movement on offense and discipline on defense. Adapting to Ginobili's special talents proved challenging but worthwhile for the Spurs coach.

"The willingness to take big shots, the willingness to do what it takes to win, and to do it at the highest possible level of intensity," said Popovich, "is there every single minute he steps on the court."

Like everyone else, Popovich watches and marvels at Ginobili and his amazing body control. It is not just his quickness that makes him special, but also his unique moves that leave opponents baffled and teammates in awe.

"When he gets into a rhythm . . . you want to sit there and watch him play," said Spurs star Tim Duncan. "You get mesmerized by what he's doing."

"He's one of the most natural players that we have in our league," says Spurs guard Brent Barry, "who can, on a nightly basis, just do some things that are flat-out amazing and jaw-dropping."

Ginobili grew up in Argentina playing hoops with his two brothers and his father, who coached basketball. He joined the Spurs after playing six pro seasons in Argentina and Italy. The 6-foot 5-inch left-hander raised his average in each of his first three NBA seasons, from 7.6 points per game in 2002–03 to 12.8 the next season and 16.0 in 2004–05. More important, he became one of the Spurs' go-to guys in the fourth quarter because of his leadership and his ability to come through in the clutch.

And Ginobili, already a national hero in Argentina, has become an NBA fan favorite as well, especially after his performance in the 2005 Playoffs. With his exciting style of play, he has made believers out of everyone, even his coach.

"The more I watched him play . . . the more I realized there was going to be a lot more good doing it his way than my way," Popovich said during the 2005 NBA Finals. "At the beginning of the [2004–05] season, we made the commitment to [turn Ginobili loose] . . . and see where it goes. And this is where it's gone."

Chris Webber

Power Forward

Mayce Edward Christopher Webber III, also known as Chris Webber, also known as C-Webb — by any name, he has been one of the NBA's best players and top power forwards since he was the number-one pick in the 1993 NBA Draft.

The 6-foot 10-inch, 245-pound Webber won the 1993–94 NBA Rookie of the Year Award and has put up impressive numbers since, averaging better than 20 points and 10 rebounds per game during his career.

Webber's parents, Mayce II and Doris, scrimped and saved to send Chris and his four younger siblings to private schools. Chris, who began playing basketball in sixth grade, shot up to 6 feet 5 inches by eighth grade and earned an academic scholarship to Detroit Country Day, a private high school in Michigan.

At first, he did not want to attend Country Day. His friends attended another high school, and Country Day required him to wear a jacket and tie every day. But he came to love the school (he remains close to his coach), and once he reached the NBA, he paid for each of his younger siblings to attend Country Day.

Webber led Country Day to three state titles in four years before moving on to the University of Michigan. He and four other freshman players at Michigan comprised the Fab Five. The talented group posted a 20–8 record and advanced to the 1992 NCAA Championship Game.

After his freshman year, Webber played on an all-star team that scrimmaged against the Dream Team. Karl Malone, maybe the greatest power forward ever, said after playing against Webber, "Let me know when he comes to the NBA, so I can retire."

After playing for Golden State and Washington in his first five seasons, Webber found a home in Sacramento.

Webber earned All-NBA honors five times during his six-plus seasons in Sacramento, including a first-team selection in 2000–01 and a second-team selection in 2001–02, when he led the Kings to the NBA's best record (61–21). He led the NBA in rebounding (13.0) in 1998–99, and finished sixth in scoring (27.1 points per game) in 2000–01.

But Webber's quest for an NBA title came up short, in frustrating fashion: The Kings ended their season with Game 7 losses in 2002, 2003, and 2004.

Webber continues his pursuit of an NBA title in Philadelphia, which acquired him from the Kings in February 2005. He has secured his place in history as one of the game's best power forwards. He just wants to hoist the NBA Championship Trophy.

"That's all I think about," said Webber. "That's what drives me. That's what I hunger for."

The NBA Finals

Holding the Larry O'Brien NBA Championship Trophy, it's what every NBA superstar dreams about. Only one team gets the chance every year, but it's what every player strives for — and the great ones never give up until they're holding the trophy in their hands.